A Pile of

Giggles 3

~ Clean Jokes...For Teens and Their Families~

Success Families

Emma, Isaac, Hanna and SherLynne Beach

A Pile of Giggles 3 -*Clean Jokes...For Teens and Their Families*
Emma, Isaac, Hanna and SherLynne Beach, Success Families
Family Joke Books Series
Copyright © 2015 Success Families, Mapleton, Utah

ISBN-13: 978-1519779014
ISBN-10: 1519779011

. ....

Dedication

To Our cousins and friends with whom we love
to share great jokes over and over!

Introduction

We love puns, jokes and silly thoughts. Everything in this book is clean, silly, and perfect for young teens and their families to tell over and over.

Illustrated by children and a mom, this book inspires drawing fun conclusions about each joke.... So here's an idea...grab a cup of milk and a plate of cookies, a drawing pad of paper and some pencils, and see what your imagination comes up with as each pun and joke is shared.

Jokes

A man wanting to borrow another man's newspaper asks, "Are you finishe(d)?"

The other man replies, "No, I'm Norwegian."

A vulture boards an airplane, carrying two dead raccoons. The stewardess looks at him and says, "I'm sorry, sir! Only one carrion allowed per passenger."

A hungry traveller stops at a monastery and is taken to the kitchens. A brother is frying chips.

'Are you the friar?' he asks.

'No. I'm the chip monk,' he replies.

Did you hear about these new reversible jackets?

I'm excited to see how they turn out.

Why did the pig stop sunbathing?

He was bacon in the heat.

Did you hear about the crime that happened in a parking garage?

It was wrong on so many levels.

Two hydrogen atoms meet. One says, "I've lost my electron".

The other says "Are you sure?"

The first replies, "Yes, I'm positive."

Did you hear about the guy who got hit in the head with a can of soda?

He was lucky it was a soft drink.

Have you ever tried to eat a clock?

It's very time consuming.

Who doesn't eat on Thanksgiving?

A turkey because it is always stuffed.

Did you hear about the Buddhist who refused Novocain during a root canal?

His goal: transcend dental medication.

A small boy swallowed some coins and was taken to a hospital.   When his grandmother telephoned to ask how he was a nurse said 'No change yet'.

What is the difference between a nicely dressed man on a tricycle and a poorly dressed man on a bicycle?

A tire.

That girl said she met me at a Vegetarian restaurant, but I never met herbivore.

Did you see the movie about the hot dog?

It was an Oscar Wiener.

What did the grape say when it got stepped on?

Nothing - but it let out a little whine.

I said to this bloke,"I'm opening a shop in the middle east."

He said,"Dubai?"

I said,"Yes, and sell."

How does the Solar System hold up its trousers?

With an asteroid belt

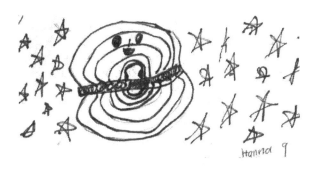

A bear walked into a restraunt and says, "I'll have a soda......and some of those fries."

The waiter says, "Why the big pause?"

What was the reporter doing at the ice cream shop?

Getting the scoop!

What's the definition of a will?

It's a dead giveaway.

What kinds of music do planets sing?

Neptunes

A woman has twins and gives them up for adoption. One of them goes to a family in Egypt and is named "Ahmal." The other goes to a family in Spain; they name him "Juan." Years later, Juan sends a picture of himself to his birth mother. Upon receiving the picture, she tells her husband that she wishes she also had a picture of Ahmal. Her husband responds, "They're twins! If you've seen Juan, you've seen Ahmal."

"What does Karl Marx put on his pasta?

Communist Manipesto!"

What do you call an alligator in a vest?

An investigator!

How do turtles talk to each other?

By using shell phones!

A vulture boards an airplane, carrying two dead raccoons. The stewardess looks at him and says, "I'm sorry, sir, only one carrion allowed per passenger."

A rubber band gun was taken away in algebra class as it was a weapon of math disruption.

What is a plumbers favorite shoes?

Clogs.

Did you hear about the chef?

He pasta-way.

Me and my friend were going to a fancy dress party. My friend said, "I'm going as a small island off the coast of Italy."

I said, "Don't be Sicily"

There was a farmer who noticed a fly buzzing around the cow's ear while he was milking it. Next thing you know, the fly was in the bucket of milk.

The farmer says, "In one ear, and out the udder!"

Why are teddy bears never hungry?

They are always stuffed!

What do you call chandeliers?

High Lights.

Where are average things made?

In the satisfactory.

So what if I don't know what apocalypse means!?

It's not the end of the world!

Why did the spider go to the computer?

To check his web site.

Where do polar bears vote?

The North Poll.

Two hydrogen atoms meet.

One says, "I've lost my electron."

The other says, "Are you sure?"

The first replies, "Yes, I'm positive."

This is a story of twin Siamese kittens, or more specifically, of their shared appendage; it is a tail of two kitties.

Darth Vader says "Luke Skywalker - I know what you're getting for Christmas. I felt your presents".

What do baseball players eat on?

Home plates!

What do you call a sleeping bull?

A bull-dozer.

What did the judge say when the skunk
walked into the court room?

Odor in the court!

Why did the turkey cross the road?

To prove he wasn't chicken!

Why do fish live in salt water?

Because pepper makes them sneeze!

How do you fix a broken tomato?

With tomato paste.

Where do you go when you feel cold in a square room?

The corners, they are always 90 degrees.

Mahatma Gandhi, walked barefoot most of
the time, which produced an impressive set
of calluses on his feet. He also ate very little,
which made him rather frail and with his odd
diet, he suffered from bad breath. This made
him...A super callused fragile mystic hexed
by halitosis.

What do you call a knight who is afraid to
fight?

Sir Render.

This bloke said to me,"I've dropped my
Scrabble set all over the road."

I said,"What's the word on the street?"

Why did the lion spit out the clown?

Because he tasted funny!

Where do polar bears vote?

The North Poll.

What's purple and 5000 miles long?

The Grape Wall of China!

A plane full of Japanese car parts has
exploded in midair today. A local
weatherman said it was raining Datsun cogs.

Why are playing cards like wolves?

They come in packs.

Police arrested a man who robbed a bank while Tweeting about it. He's hoping for a short sentence.

A dog gave birth to puppies near the road and was cited for littering.

A former Miss Russia has been arrested for both shoplifting and counterfeiting. Police say she can't get her bearings straight.

What do you get when you cross a snake and a pie?

A pie-thon!

There was a scare in the Middle East when famous political figure, Ali Ali was hospitalized because of a dangerously high amount of toxins in his bloodstream. After 5 hours of surgery and blood transfusions, everything is all right now because he is Ali Ali, toxin free.

An appeals court has upheld a ban on pitbulls. That's another victory in the war on terrier.

Why are fish so smart?

Because they live in schools.

What do you get from a pampered cow?

Spoiled milk

Evidence has been found that William Tell and his family were avid bowlers. However, all league records were unfortunately lost, so we'll never know for whom the Tells bowled.

I was arrested at the airport. Just because I was greeting my cousin Jack!

All that I said was "Hi Jack", but very loud.

An Indian chief had three wives. The first wife slept on cowhide, the second wife a deerhide and the third on hippopotamus hide. The first gave birth to a baby boy, the second to a baby girl and the third had twins - a boy and a girl. Looking at what happened, the old chief declared, "The squaw on the hippopotamus is equal to the sum of the squaws on the other two hides!"

A man leaned to his right because his right leg was shorter than his left. He finally went to see a surgeon after much insistence from friends.

Later, one of those friends saw the man walking down the street and noticed that the man's legs were exactly the same length. "See, what did I tell you?", the friend boasted. "You didn't believe the doctor could fix your leg!"

The man said, "I stand corrected."

What did the Tin Man say when he got run over by a steamroller?

"Curses! Foil again!"

A woman was driving in her car on a narrow road. She was knitting at the same time, so she was driving very slowly.

A man came up from behind and he wanted to pass her. He opened the window and yelled, "Pull over! Pull over!"

The lady yelled back, "No, it's a sweater!"

What do prisoners use to call each other?

Cell phones.

Two friends meet and one of them says:"I've taught my dog how to speak English!"

"That's impossible", says the other man."Dogs don't speak!"

"It's true! I'll show you." He turns to his dog, "How's the situation in England?" The dog answers: "Rough, rough."

How does a spoiled rich girl change a lightbulb?

She says, "Daddy, I want a new apartment."

One day an English grammar teacher was looking ill. A student asked, "What's the matter?"

"Tense," answered the teacher, describing how he felt.

The student paused, then continued, "What was the matter? What has been the matter? What might have been the matter?"

What do you get when you cross a snowman with a vampire?

Frostbite.

Where do you find a no legged dog?

Right where you left him.

What lies at the bottom of the ocean and twitches?

A nervous wreck.

Teacher: Rumiko, be careful your purse is open. Someone might take your money!

Rumiko: Oh, no. I left it open so I can get more money.

Teacher: How can you get more money?

Rumiko: The weather report said we would have some change in our weather!

Boyfriend: What is your favorite music group?

Girlfriend: I love U2!

Boyfriend: I love you too, but what is your favorite music group?

Two Eskimos, out to fish in their canoe got cold and decided to build a small fire in the bottom of their canoe to keep warm. Of course the boat caught fire and sank, proving that you can't have your kayak and heat it too.

Why are there so many Smiths in the phone book?

They all have phones.

A group of chess enthusiasts checked into a hotel and were standing in the lobby discussing their recent tournament victories. After about an hour, the manager came out of the office and asked them to disperse.

"But why?" they asked, as they moved off.

"Because," he said, "I can't stand chess-nuts boasting in an open foyer."

I hear this new cemetery is very popular. People are just dying to get in.

Why do bagpipers walk when they play?

They're trying to get away from the noise.

One day a man went to see the Mozart's tomb. When he got there, the tomb was open and Mozart was sitting there tearing up pieces of paper.

The men asked: "What are you doing with all of your great works of music?"

Mozart replied, "I'm decomposing!".

What do you call four bull fighters in quicksand?

Quatro sinko.

What do you call cheese that isn't yours?

Nacho Cheese.

There is this man who meets a fairy. He is granted three wishes. Having wished for his most urgent needs the man uses his third wish to ask the fairy to return and give him three more wishes. The fairy complies and says: "You can call me whenever you want." "How can I call you. Please tell me your name." the man says. "My name is Nuff," says the fairy. "Well", says the man "That is an odd name. I have never heard of it before." The fairy replies, "Surely you will have heard of Fairy Nuff." (fair enough)

What has four legs, is big, green, fuzzy, and if it fell out of a tree would kill you?

A pool table.

[This one works best when spoken aloud.] Once upon a time a mother skunk had two children named "In" and "Out". They were very active children and whenever In was in, Out was out. When Out was in, In was out.

One day when Out was in and In was out, the mother skunk said "Out, go out and find In and tell In to come in."

Out went out to find In to bring In back in. Within a minute, Out came back in from going out and Out brought In right back in.

Amazed, the mother skunk said, "Out, you just went out to find In and brought In right back in! How did you do it?"

To this, Out replied "Instinct!" [In stinked]

In London, one man to another:

A: "You know, my daughter has married an Irishman"

B: "Oh, really?"

A: "No, O'Reilly"

A man walks into 7-11 with a lizard on his shoulder. He walks up to the cashier and asks for a big gulp for himself and a slurpie for Tiny, his lizard. The cashier looks a little taken aback but serves him and Tiny.

Finally, curiosity gets the better of him; "Why do you call him Tiny?"

The man replies,"Because he's my newt."

A: How do you like your new job at the cemetery?

B: I quit after a week. I found the work too frustrating.

A: What happened?

B: No matter what I said to the customers, they were always dead right!

How do crazy people go through the forest?

They take the psycho path.

What do you get from a pampered cow?

Spoiled milk.

There were two spies escaping from the enemy over the Alps into neutral Switzerland during the war. As they began to feel safe, one spy starts to tell the other what he found out in enemy territory. The other tells him to speak quietly.

"Why?", asks his friend a little perplexed. "There's nobody around for miles. I could scream and not a soul would hear us up here.....!"

"Ah," replied the other, "haven't you heard? There are mountain ears?"   (mountaineers)

Did you hear about the guy that lost his left arm and leg in a car crash?

He's all right now.

Sources

http://punjokes.com/#sthash.lykbhZsi.dpuf

http://www.funenglishgames.com/funstuff/funnypuns.html

http://www.funny2.com/punsb.htm

http://www.jokes4us.com/peoplejokes/funnyacronyms.html

http://www.punoftheday.com

http://www.rd.com/jokes/puns/

http://www.sliptalk.com

More Available

By SherLynne Beach

and SuccessFamilies.com

- Powerful Mind: A class workbook for adults and children
- Mind Chatter Mastery Course
- Timeless Principles Of Raising Great Kids: Discover timeless wisdom, seemingly magical secrets to building strong families and a practical, ... best-selling authors & mentors
- Cursive Jokes Copywork 1: Write and Laugh!
- Manuscript Jokes Copywork 1: Write and Laugh
- Proverbs for Children: Handwriting, Copy-Work and Memorization (Volume 2)
- Simple Outlines Workbook: Trackable Progress K-3 Short Compositions Practice Workbook 1 of 3 (Writing Series).
- Simple Rough Drafts Workbook: Writing Steps Series, 2nd of 3 books (Volume 2)
- Simple Final Drafts Workbook: Trackable Progress K-3 Short Compositions Practice Workbook 2 of 3
- A Pile of Giggles 1, 2 and 3 (jokes and puns)

More SuccessFamilies
Books and Courses
Coming in 2016

- Silly Spelling Practice
- Thinking Through Books –Basic Reports (inspired by the Ben Carson Story)
- Classics Reading List –Pocket Book
- I AM in Charge Of My Mind Series, Journals and Workbooks and Courses
- I AM in Charge of my Emotions Series, Let Go and Heal Journals, Workbooks and Instruction
- Family Joke Books
- Children's Books
- And MORE!

Made in the USA
Middletown, DE
19 December 2018